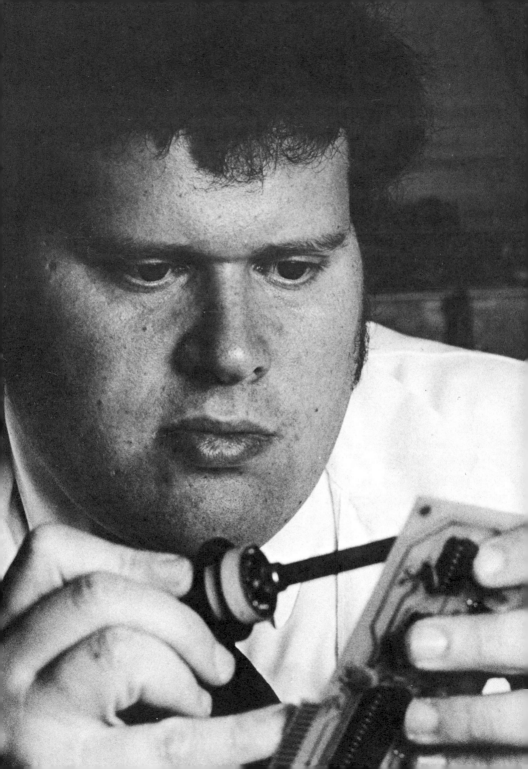

Jerrold Petrofsky

Biomedical Pioneer

by Timothy R. Gaffney

 CHILDRENS PRESS, CHICAGO

PICTURE ACKNOWLEDGMENTS

Philip and Jeanette Petrofsky—52 (2 photos), 53
Wright State University—2, 10, 22, 55, 56, 57, 58, 59, 64, 84, 92, 98, 99, 100
Timothy R. Gaffney—54, 97
Cover illustration by David J. Catrow. Photograph of Jerrold Petrofsky on page 2
 and the photograph on page 10 of Nan Davis and Dr. Petrofsky standing in the
 lab are from Wright State University.

Library of Congress Cataloging in Publication Data

Gaffney, Timothy R.
 Jerrold Petrofsky, biomedical pioneer.

 Summary: Discusses the achievements of a scientist at
Wright State University who has learned to use electronic
stimulation to help people paralyzed after spinal cord
injuries recover enough to move and even walk again.
 1. Petrofsky, Jerrold Scott—Juvenile literature.
2. Biomedical engineers—United States—Biography—
Juvenile literature. [1. Petrofsky, Jerrold Scott.
2. Biomedical engineering. 3. Physically handicapped.
4. Physical therapy. 5. Spinal cord—Wounds and injuries]
I. Title.
R856.2.P48G34 1984   617'.307'0924 [B]   83-25268
ISBN 0-516-03201-1

 2 3 4 5 6 7 8 9 10 R 93 92 91 90 89 88 87 86 85 '

DEDICATION

To Kim

ACKNOWLEDGMENTS

This book would not have been possible without the enthusiastic cooperation of Jerrold Petrofsky, Ph.D., and Nanette Davis. It was conceived by Jean Gaffney, my wife. The following people helped in a variety of ways: Susan Steele; Jeffrey Housh; Steven Petrofsky; Chandler Phillips, M.D.; Roger M. Glaser, Ph.D.; Harry H. Heaton III; Debra M. Hendershot; Carol Siyahi; Larry Kinneer; Russell Cook; and Jan Hofmann.

FOREWARD

This book describes experiments that use electrical stimulation to exercise paralyzed muscles. The experiments are conducted under closely supervised conditions by scientists with extensive medical training. Electricity can be deadly; never use it in experiments without adequate training and supervision.

Table of Contents

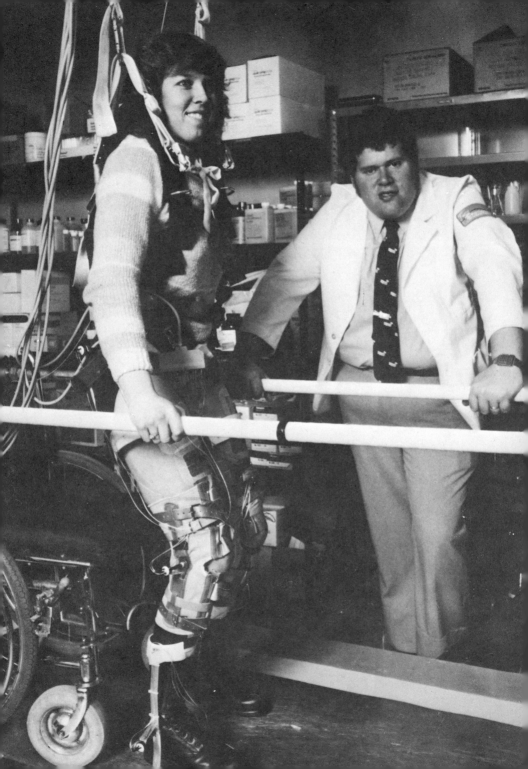

Chapter 1

THE FIRST STEPS

The date is November 11, 1982. On a Midwest college campus, news photographers crowd into a cluttered electronics laboratory. They jostle each other for camera angles. Those who come in last stand on tables or chairs in the back of the lab. A TV camera feeds a view of the scene to the next room. Here reporters from all over the United States and several other countries watch.

All eyes and cameras are on a young blond woman sitting in a wheelchair on a low platform. Her legs are almost hidden in tangles of wires and straps. Black paratrooper boots cover her feet. Low handrails run along each side of the platform. From a long rail above the platform hangs a parachute harness. The woman is strapped into it.

Six paces in front of the woman stands a rack of electronic equipment connected by countless strands of colored wire. In the jumble of equipment is a small computer. Several black cables stretch from the equipment to the woman. She is wired to the computer.

A large, ruddy-cheeked man in a blue suit stands by the computer. He watches the woman closely, his hand at the keyboard. He says, "Look at me, Nan." Nanette Davis, the woman in the wheelchair, gives him all her attention. The photographers raise their cameras, but she ignores them.

"High voltage on," the man says. "Power coming up." Nan grasps the handrails. Lab assistants kneel on each side of the platform, watching her feet. The man begins a countdown: "Three, two, one—power up." Nan leans forward and her legs push her up from the wheelchair.

The photographers fire their flashguns. The sounds of shutters and motor drives fill the room. Paraplegic Nan Davis, who has not had the use of her legs in more than four years, is standing. Part of her weight is supported by the parachute harness, but most of her weight is on her feet.

"OK, all set?" the man asks. "Right leg coming up." Nan Davis, paralyzed from the waist down, takes a step.

"Left leg coming up." Another step. Nan holds on to the handrails for balance. The technicians follow her feet. Her steps are slow and clumsy, but each one brings her closer to the end of the platform.

"Right leg, left leg." A shuffle. "Right leg up." Another step. "Left leg forward. Right leg forward."

Finally she reaches the end of the platform. Six impossible steps on paralyzed legs.

More than four years earlier, an automobile accident had left Nan with a broken back and a damaged spinal cord. While she lay helpless in a hospital bed, doctors and nurses told her she would never again be able to use her legs—

never again ride a bike, never again run, never again walk.

She refused to believe them. She clung to a hope that someday, somehow, somebody would find a way for her to use her legs again.

Now it has happened.

Her accomplishment makes Nan the center of attention. But in a meeting with reporters afterward, she nods towards the man in the blue suit and tells them, "What I knew all along was going to happen someday did. This man did it."

The man's name: Jerrold S. Petrofsky.

Jerrold Petrofsky is executive director of the National Center for Rehabilitation Engineering at Wright State University in Dayton, Ohio, and a professor of biomedical engineering. Biomedical engineers take the tools and ideas of engineering and use them in medicine. Through their research, biomedical scientists like Petrofsky have learned that the human body in many ways acts just like a machine.

Petrofsky had been fascinated by this fact for years. His studies have always mixed the areas of biology and engineering. He was studying biology in college and working part time as a computer repairman in 1969 when he noticed how much the computer's internal wiring looked like the human body's nervous system. Working with Nan, he was to prove his theories.

Some of the biological machinery in Nan Davis's body is broken. The accident on her high school graduation night in

1978 broke her back and damaged her spinal cord. The injury to her spinal cord left her paralyzed from the ribs down.

Nan isn't alone. About half a million people in the United States are paralyzed because of spinal cord injuries—mostly from automobile accidents, sports injuries, and gunshot wounds. About fifteen thousand Americans are paralyzed each year. The number of people around the world who are paralyzed from spinal cord injuries is far greater. For all of these people, their injuries are like jail sentences that confine them to wheelchairs for the rest of their lives.

Around the world, medical scientists are trying to learn why the body seems unable to heal injuries like Nan's the way it heals cuts and bruises. They have made some progress, but so far they have not come up with a foolproof cure for spinal cord injuries.

Petrofsky is trying to perfect an alternative. Instead of letting people sit in wheelchairs waiting for a cure, he wants to get them out now. He has found a way to do it—with computers.

Chapter 2

JERRY

The second child of Philip and Jeanette Petrofsky was born on May 5, 1948, in St. Louis, Missouri. Jerrold Scott Petrofsky had one brother, two-year-old Steven.

The Petrofskys lived in a house built in 1880 on Cleveland Avenue. It was the same house the Petrofsky family had occupied since the 1920s: a large, Victorian-era home on a pleasant neighborhood street. The boys and their parents lived downstairs, and their grandparents lived upstairs. Jeanette and Philip Petrofsky live there still.

Jerry showed an interest in mechanical things from the very start. His mother recalled that one day "He had a little robot that would wind up and go like crazy all over the place." As she remembered, it was one of his favorite toys.

But perhaps it was natural for both boys to take an interest in mechanical and electrical things. They were born at the dawn of a new era. Jets, rockets, and nuclear power were just being developed. Television was new and not in very many homes. Transistors had not yet replaced vacuum tubes, and microcomputers were still the stuff of wild science fiction stories.

Also, their father had served in World War II as a radar

technician. During part of his sons' formative years he had a job rebuilding electrical motors.

Jerry was just three years old when his father took a night school course in electronics to prepare for that job. Philip would hold the boy on his lap while he worked on the electronics projects the course required. The preschooler watched his father's hands in fascination. It was Jerry's introduction to a complex world and his fascination with this world would never fade.

As the boys grew older, they began to work on their own projects. They built crystal radio sets. When transistor radios appeared, they took parts from broken sets to build working ones.

Their favorite store was a Goodwill store that sold broken radios and TV sets for pennies. While they were still in grade school, Steve and Jerry explored the world of electronics by buying old TVs and radios, tearing into them, and making them work. Sometimes they sold them and made money.

The Petrofskys wanted their sons to learn about science. They weren't wealthy, but they made sure the boys had lots of books to read, and they bought them a chemistry set.

Mrs. Petrofsky wasn't always certain she and her husband were doing the right thing. The chemistry set especially worried her. "I was always afraid he was going to blow the house up," she said of Jerry.

Both boys seemed to soak up information, but Jerry in particular showed an unquenchable thirst for knowledge. His parents noticed that he had an unusual ability to grasp ideas quickly. His curiosity knew no bounds, and he dived into one activity after another.

Jerry began school at Sherman Elementary. When he was in the fourth grade, all the students took an I.Q. test to determine their intelligence. Every student who scored 140 or higher was placed in a special educational program for gifted students at Mullanphy Elementary School. Jerry was among them. He went to Mullanphy for one year, then finished elementary school in a similar program at Wade Elementary.

The program, as he would say later, was "tough." He had "at least seven or eight hours" of homework every night. His mother said he was sometimes at his books until two in the morning. She worried that it was too much for such a young child, but Jerry devoured his lessons.

He took art lessons at the art museum, music lessons at the St. Louis Symphony. "By the time I left grade school I was speaking German and French, playing four musical instruments, and I was fairly good in sculpture," he said.

With all that, he still had enough free time to be a Cub Scout and Boy Scout, learn photography, and pursue his interest in electronics. When the U.S. Federal Communications Commission approved CB (citizens band) radios, Jerry,

Steve, and some of their friends bought radio kits and built them. They were among the first in the country to be licensed CB radio operators.

The boys weren't content just to build kits, though. They were forever making their own changes, boosting power, or rigging up some special device. Sometimes it caused trouble.

Jerry recalls when Steve installed their CB radio in his bedroom. They had been sharing one bedroom, but Steve had decided he needed his own room. He had moved out and taken over what had been their photographic darkroom (which, once upon a time, had been their father's den). Steve had run a cable from the CB radio in his room to the antenna on the house roof.

Unfortunately, the boys had not yet learned about lightning rods.

When thunderstorms swept over the city, the CB antenna attracted electricity. Lightning never struck the house, but sometimes electrical charges would build up in the antenna until huge sparks leaped across Steve's room from the cable to a radiator. Anyone outside the room would hear a startling "Crack! Crack! Crack!" as the sparks flew.

They never burned down the house, but once Jerry thought it was coming down on top of him. The house, today more than one hundred years old, had settled and sagged. The old walls and ceilings, made of wooden strips (called laths) and covered with plaster, were strained. Late one night when

Jerry was in bed, he heard a strange rumbling sound. The next instant, the ceiling fell down on him! All the old plaster had worked loose and had finally given way in one big chunk. But Jerry wasn't hurt, and his father put in a new ceiling the next weekend.

After elementary school, Jerry attended Southwest High School, which also had a program for gifted students. But Jerry found the work there less demanding. That left him with enough idle time to get into trouble.

No one doubted that he was bright—certainly not the teacher he had for physics during his sophomore year. As he described it later, she was a biology teacher who had been reassigned owing to a shortage of physics teachers. As it seemed to him then and still seems to him now, Jerry knew more about physics than she did.

The result was that Jerry started conducting his own impish experiments in the back of the physics lab.

One day he found bottles of ammonium hydroxide and hydrochloric acid. He knew the properties of those two chemical compounds, and his mind leaped to a wonderful idea. "If you take the two and mix them together, it forms ammonium chloride, which is a white solid," he explained later. He took the bottles to the back of the lab, placed a fan behind them—and took off the caps.

A white, foglike cloud erupted, rolled across the lab, and spread throughout the building. The cloud was actually fine white powder, and it covered everything. "That didn't go over too well," he said. He was ordered to clean up the mess.

Another time he became fascinated with the electrical equipment in the lab—especially the Van de Graaff generator.

A Van de Graaff generator is a device that generates large charges of static electricity. It is often used in schools to show how electricity works. It doesn't make enough current to hurt someone seriously, but it can deliver enough voltage to make a person's hair stand on end.

The machine was stored after class with other valuable equipment in a locked, wire-mesh cage. Jerry, who was a lab assistant, decided to wire the generator to the cage and put a timer on it. "Ten minutes after closing the cage and locking the door, the Van de Graaff would kick on and energize the cage with 10 million volts," he said. "There wasn't enough current to hurt you, but it sure made you jump." He insists it was not a booby trap, but just an experiment. And besides, it surrounded the cage with a pretty blue glow when it came on.

Things came to a head one day in Jerry's second semester. His besieged physics teacher was trying to teach electronics to the class. As he recalled, she knew almost nothing about transistors, while he knew quite a bit. She found him correcting her constantly in front of the other students. Finally, she had enough. She stopped the class and told Jerry that if he was so all-fired smart, *he* could give the lecture on electronics.

"I said, 'Fine.' And I went up and started giving the lecture," he said. "So she talked to me afterward and said, rather than being in the back of the class blowing things up, would I want to give all the lectures on radio." From then on, he was an assistant high school teacher—a good preparation for an eventual career as a college professor.

During their summer vacations, both Jerry and Steve worked at Camp Hawthorne, a summer camp operated by the St. Louis Jewish Community Center at Lake of the Ozarks in central Missouri. They both worked as kitchen boys, but later Steve became a camp truck driver and Jerry worked as an administrative assistant.

Their summers away from home made both boys more independent, their mother said. It also brought them needed money. "That money they earned helped them get through college," she said.

Dr. Petrofsky's Bioengineering Laboratory at Wright State
University reflects his life-long interest in manufacturing
electronic devices made from odds and ends of other pieces
of equipment.

Chapter 3

THE BODY COMPUTER

Being older, Steve started college first. He wanted to be an electrical engineer, and he enrolled at the Missouri School of Mines and Metallurgical Engineering in Rolla, Missouri. (The school is now part of the University of Missouri.) Jerry joined Steve there to study chemical engineering after graduating from high school in 1966.

Rolla, as they refer to the school, was very good and very tough. In Jerry's opinion, it was also the dullest place on planet earth. Forty-five hundred engineering students, almost all of them male, had to share the student union's one pool table and one TV set, Jerry said later. The small town had one pizza parlor. He said he made good grades there simply because there was nothing else to do but study.

After his freshman year, he applied for a scholarship at Washington University back in St. Louis. By that time he had also developed a strong interest in biology. He and his brother began to part ways. While Steve went on to earn a master's degree in electrical engineering, Jerry took up the study of living things.

Despite all his experience in electronics, Jerry Petrofsky didn't encounter computers until the summer before his senior year at Washington University. In 1969, computers were still very big, very expensive, and very rare.

His introduction came in a physiology lab at another school, St. Louis University. Petrofsky needed a summer job, and he had learned that the lab had a computer that needed servicing. Without hesitation, he offered to do it. "I never said I didn't know how to work on them," Petrofsky admitted. "But they never really asked me, either."

The computer in question was a 1959 model Digital Equipment Corporation (DEC) machine called the LINC. It was considered a mini-computer, but it was still the size of a large refrigerator. Petrofsky had to learn how it worked—fast. He went to DEC's offices in Chicago and spent a week learning to read the company's circuit drawings. Once he understood the computer's circuitry, the rest—for him—was easy.

(As a matter of fact, Petrofsky is now one of the few people in the world who still knows how to operate the LINC. The circuitry of the machine is so outdated that its manufacturer no longer trains employees how to service it. The university let him take the machine with him when he left, since nobody else could keep it running. On indefinite loan, the LINC today stands in his Wright State lab.)

At the same time he was working on the computer, Petrofsky was studying comparative anatomy at Washington University. Perhaps the drawings in the anatomy books—drawings that showed the bones and muscles and nerves of the human body—were on his mind when he removed one of the blue side panels from the computer.

Inside was a thick bundle of wires running down the machine. From the main bundle branched smaller bundles, each wire eventually leading to some hidden interior part of the machine.

It looked just like what he had seen in anatomy books. The computer had its own equivalent of a spinal cord.

In fact, both computers and humans have nervous systems that function in much the same way.

Like the signals that a computer sends from its central processing unit through circuits to various parts of its system, human nerve signals are electrical—tiny, fast waves of electrical impulses that ripple down the nerves in the spinal cord from the brain to the rest of the body.

The body can even be thought of as a kind of robot. Real robots—the mechanical arms in automobile assembly plants or the household kind that roll around and talk—have joints and motors that enable them to move. Humans have joints and muscles. In both cases, movement is controlled by signals from the brain—the computer's electronic one or the human's biological one.

Petrofsky wasn't the first person to notice these things. But he saw that if the systems inside humans and computers are so similar, then there could be ways to combine the two.

25

Petrofsky had other work to keep him busy during his senior year, but that striking similarity between human anatomy and computers stayed with him.

For his senior class biology project, however, he had to turn his mind to something else—bats.

He had by chance met Dr. Louis D'Agrosa, a scientist (now deceased) who studied those most curious mammals. Bats are ugly little creatures, but there is much to learn from them. Among other things, they have the ability to fly in darkness by using echoes of their high-pitched chirps to guide them. They hibernate in cold weather; that is, their bodies begin to operate much more slowly, and their hearts beat at only a fraction of their normal speed.

Petrofsky's project under D'Agrosa was to study the heart rates and body temperatures of bats. All he needed was a cave and four thousand live bats. No problem.

For a controlled setting where he could study the bats, he got permission to use one of several cavernous underground vaults that belonged to the university. They had been government ammunition bunkers during World War II and now stood empty. He got a state permit to collect bats, had himself vaccinated against rabies in case a diseased bat bit him, and set off to hunt bats. Once he had collected a large jar full of the little black, sharp-toothed creatures, he would take them home and store them overnight in his mother's refrigerator until he could take them to the vault.

His mother must have loved her son very much.

"He said everything would be fine as long as the bats stayed cool," she said later. "He said they would just sleep, and that was true. But we were always very cautious whenever we opened the refrigerator door." Fortunately, none of the bats ever got loose, either in the house or in the refrigerator.

After earning a bachelor's degree in biology, Petrofsky began studying physiology at St. Louis University Medical School. He received a Ph.D. degree in physiology from St. Louis in 1974. That same year he was married to Cheryl Carey. Cheryl was teaching first grade at Jana Elementary School in Hazelwood, a St. Louis suburb.

It was in his physiological studies that he began to merge all he had learned about the human body and electronics.

Chapter 4

THE HUMAN ROBOT

People have been trying since ancient times to understand the mechanism called the human body. One of its great mysteries was those things under the skin that bulged and hardened during exercise. It was obvious that muscles made the body work, but nobody knew how muscles themselves worked.

Several thousand years ago, Greeks and Romans thought muscles were like hollow bags. They knew that blood vessels were hollow tubes that carried fluid (blood) to the muscles. They decided that nerves also had to be like hollow tubes that delivered some substance to the muscles. They called that substance "animal spirits." When a person wanted to bend an arm, they thought, the brain would send animal spirits into the biceps—that large muscle on the front of the upper arm. As the spirits poured in, the muscle would bulge in the middle and both ends would come closer together. The result was muscle contraction.

The idea was all wrong, of course, but many experiments were conducted, as recently as the 1600s, in attempts to discover if animal spirits were solid or liquid.

That thinking eventually changed as people learned more about the body. As scientists began to study electricity, they began to suspect that *it*, not some mysterious solid or fluid, made muscles work. After all, people had long known that the shock of an electric eel could make muscles jerk.

In the 1780s, an Italian scientist named Luigi Galvani conducted a famous experiment to demonstrate that nerves did indeed carry electricity. Opening the back of a frog, Galvani touched one end of an iron rod to its spinal cord and the other end to a lower leg muscle. The muscle contracted!

Later experiments showed that Galvani had made a mistake. It was a chemical reaction of the flesh to the metals in the rod, not the short-circuiting of the nervous system, that made the muscle contract. But he proved his idea by touching the nerve of one frog directly to the muscle of another, producing the same kind of contraction. After Galvani's work, electricity in the body became the subject of much scientific study.

Unfortunately, it also became the tool of many unscientific quacks. They promoted electricity as a cure-all for everything from arthritis to heart disease. The public, and scientists as well, turned against the idea that electricity could cure anything.

That made it more difficult for those who wanted to study electrical stimulation of muscles to be taken seriously. It wasn't until the early 1960s that scientists began to make meaningful advances. A few, working separately from one another at universities scattered around the world, were trying to use electricity to unlock paralyzed muscles by the time Petrofsky entered the field.

It isn't hard to make a muscle contract. All you need are a muscle, some electricity, and a pair of electrodes to apply it. But the human nervous system is not like household electric current, and muscles go through a complex set of actions when they work.

Nerves that stimulate muscles have end plates that distribute the stimulation over thousands of individual muscle fibers. Those branches distribute nerve impulses through the muscle so that different parts of the muscle are stimulated at different times. What appears to be the contraction of one large muscle is actually the alternate contracting and relaxing of several small subdivisions of that muscle. Any electrical stimulation technique that reproduces that coordinated action requires several electrodes, each delivering impulses at just the right voltage and frequency and in just the right order. And all of that is required just to make one muscle behave. Getting an arm or a leg to move requires the coordinated control of several groups of muscles.

Petrofsky was aware of these problems. But he was also aware of a new invention that could change the whole picture—the microcomputer.

A microcomputer is a complete computer on a chip of silicon smaller than a fingernail. The device, correctly called a microprocessor, is at the heart of every home computer and video game machine. Microcomputers made computers far smaller than ever before, and far cheaper as well. Microcomputers seem to be almost everywhere now, but in the mid-1970s the first models were just coming out of the factories.

A computer can control the movement in a leg because it operates much faster than nerves and muscles. A muscle's contraction is measured by the thousandth of a second (millisecond); computers operate by the billionth of a second (nanosecond). A computer can monitor several muscles, calculate what each is doing, and decide what to make them do next in much less time than a millisecond.

Petrofsky found that a microcomputer, properly programmed, could handle the task of delivering electrical stimulation to produce smooth contraction and relaxation of muscles.

In one experiment involving a laboratory cat, he used his own nerve signals to control one of the animal's legs. He attached sensors to the surface of one of his legs in several places and wired them to the computer. He did the same thing to one leg on the cat, using electrodes instead of sensors. When he moved his leg, the sensors monitored the electrical activity in his muscles and sent the signals to the computer. The computer then translated the signals into electrical impulses and sent them to the electrodes on the cat's leg. The electrodes sent pulses of electricity into the cat's muscles, and the leg moved. When Petrofsky bent his leg, the cat's leg bent; when he straightened his leg, the cat's leg straightened. In between was the computer.

The work was interesting, but of no great importance to the world at large. That changed one day in 1974 when Petrofsky ate what could be called the most important hamburger of his life.

To be accurate, the hamburger itself wasn't important. but while eating a triple-decker-with-everything in the medical school cafeteria one day, he discussed his research with Lawrence Salzburg, a medical student with a Ph.D. in cell physiology. And what Salzburg had to say while they munched on burgers changed Petrofsky's life.

"He suggested to me that if I could control movement [in muscles], I could help people who were paralyzed." Suddenly, Petrofsky realized the importance of his work. It could return to people the use of paralyzed limbs. It could free people from wheelchairs.

That has been his goal ever since.

Chapter 5

EARLY WORK

Petrofsky continued his work at St. Louis University until 1979, doing postdoctoral work, teaching physiology as an associate professor, and working toward a degree in computer engineering at night. A daughter, Melissa, was born to the Petrofskys on February 16, 1976.

In 1979 he transferred to Wright State University, where he became an associate professor of physiology and biomedical engineering. What drew him to Wright State was a scientist there who also was studying how muscles work.

Dr. Chandler A. Phillips was a medical doctor and an engineer. He had joined Wright State to set up the university's biomedical engineering program. His area of research was the heart muscle and how it is affected by heart diseases.

In 1976 Petrofsky visited Dayton, Ohio, to give a seminar on his research. He had not met Phillips and he had never heard of Wright State. A friend who thought their work had a lot in common took Petrofsky to meet Phillips in Phillips's campus office. "I talked to Chandler for the better part of an hour or two. We decided to get back together to do a little more talking because we had a lot of common interests in a lot of different ways," Petrofsky said later. Not only were both studying muscles, but both loved engineering and both were amateur ("ham") radio operators.

They began visiting each other and comparing notes on their research. Phillips would fly to St. Louis (he is a licensed pilot) and spend the night with the Petrofskys, sleeping on the couch.

One evening in 1977, they went to the waterfront where the Mississippi River flows through the city. They both like dixieland jazz, so they listened to a dixieland band playing on the *Robert E. Lee* riverboat. They began talking about their work again, and that evening they decided to work together. For the next two years they spent many evenings on their shortwave radios, discussing their work. Finally, Petrofsky decided to switch to Wright State. With a cubbyhole office, a laboratory, and a team of research associates, graduate students, and technicians, he continued his research with Phillips.

Their laboratory looked like a conglomeration of science lab, electronics repair service, and hobby shop. On a typical day, the benches in the lab were piled high with jumbles of electronic parts. Circuit boards and soldering irons lay everywhere. Strange-looking devices sprouted strands of wire in all directions.

Petrofsky used equipment he found in the bargain bins of electronics stores. He used cast-off wiring from the telephone company. He accepted donations whenever they were

Jerrold Petrofsky (left) and Chandler Phillips monitor experiments in the laboratory. Dr. Petrofsky has developed an active physical therapy program for paralyzed people.

offered, and when the lab was short on computers he would bring his own personal computer from home. Electrical stimulation research at that time didn't attract much attention, and funds were scarce. Much of Petrofsky's research money came from the Spinal Cord Society and the American Paralysis Association, two private organizations that encourage spinal cord injury research. Still he operated on a shoestring, and wherever he could save some money, he did.

At the same time, he knew that his work didn't require strange or exotic equipment. The microcomputers he was using carried one of the most familiar brand names of home computers in the world—Apple. Many of the special devices he built to be used with the Apples were made of parts from local hobby electronics stores. He believes scientists are just starting to learn the things they can do with the technology already available.

In the midst of all the tables and shelves of equipment, they set out to move Petrofsky's work to the next phase. That was to get paralyzed limbs not just to move, but to move with purpose.

Think of the body as a robot again. How does a robot arm move? When the computer gives the order, it sends a series of electrical signals through wires to the motors in the arm. If it's a very sophisticated arm, it may have motion sensors in it that send back signals to the computer, telling it just how much and in what direction the arm is moving. This exchange of signals, which gives the computer moment-by-moment control over the robot arm, is called feedback.

The human system works in much the same way. Its computer is that lump of gray matter called the brain. The robot arm is a human arm—or leg, for that matter—and the wires that connect it are the nerves.

When you want to move an arm, your brain sends the thought "move," in the form of electrical impulses, down to the arm through three related systems of nerves. First the impulses travel along the cranial nerves in the brain. The cranial nerves transfer the impulses to the spinal nerves, and the spinal nerves pass it on to the peripheral nerves.

The peripheral nervous system includes a variety of different kinds of nerves. The peripheral nerves that carry signals to the muscles are the motor nerves. Motor nerves end in plates that lie against the muscles. When the nerve impulses reach the end plates, a chemical reaction takes place that stimulates the muscles to contract.

Well, how does a muscle contract? If it isn't an inflatable bag, just what is it?

Skeletal muscles are actually groups of long cells. Inside the cells are bunches of fiberlike objects called myofibrils. When a nerve impulse reaches a muscle, it causes a chemical reaction inside the cells that, in turn, causes the myofibrils to slide together and overlap. That's what makes the muscle grow shorter and thicker.

The biceps muscle, like many others, is attached to bone at each end—one end to a bone in the forearm called the radius, the other end to the shoulder blade. As the biceps contracts, it pulls the forearm toward the shoulder, causing the arm to bend at the elbow.

The peripheral nervous system also includes other kinds of nerves called sensory nerves. Sensory nerves give us our own version of the robot's feedback system. Each sensory nerve has a receptor on the end that is sensitive to one kind of stimulation or another. Chemical receptors give us our senses of taste and smell; light receptors, called photo-receptors, allow us to see; pain receptors warn us when we are being hurt; and mechanical receptors sense touch, pressure, balance, and movement. Muscles, tendons, and joints contain receptors that monitor motion and send information back through the spinal cord to the brain.

Here's an experiment. Close your eyes and let both arms hang at your sides. Now, with your eyes closed, raise one arm and touch the tip of your forefinger to your nose.

You can do it without looking because of your body's feedback control system. (If you were standing, notice that your body also didn't fall flat when you closed your eyes. It kept itself balanced—another example of feedback control.)

Petrofsky's group couldn't just start working with human test subjects. They had to develop their ideas into a working system first, then prove it could be tested on people safely.

Using cats for their experiments, they designed a special harness for the rear legs. Their goal was to get a cat to walk on a treadmill, controlling its rear legs with a computer.

They placed motion sensors at several points along the cat's legs to give the computer feedback control. As the computer sent out signals to make the cat's legs move, it monitored the movement with the sensors. If a leg began to rise a bit too fast, the computer would adjust its rate of stimulation and slow the leg down. If a muscle showed weakening response to the impulses, the computer would step up the voltage to strengthen the response.

After much testing, the system worked. Petrofsky was convinced the same kind of system would work on humans, too. If he were right, it would mean that thousands of people paralyzed by spinal cord injuries might be able to walk.

Not every kind of paralysis would respond to Petrofsky's methods, though. In muscular dystrophy, for example, the muscles themselves are damaged. The muscle is simply not there to respond to stimulation. But the situation is different in cases of spinal cord injuries.

For brain signals to reach muscles, and for sensory signals to reach the brain, the nerve impulses must travel through the body's main wiring harness—the spinal cord. If anything happens to damage the spinal cord, those signals may be blocked. The result, for the part of the body cut off from the brain, is paralysis.

The nerve pathway to the muscles may be blocked, but there is nothing wrong with the muscles themselves. As long as the motor nerves that go into the muscles are undamaged, the muscles are still able to respond to stimulation.

By April of 1982, Petrofsky had received the university's approval to use human subjects in tests. A special chair called a leg trainer was designed and built for the tests. Near the bottom of the chair, a cuff that fit around a leg was attached to a rope-and-pulley weight-lifting system. This would allow the scientists to measure how much work an electrically stimulated leg could do.

Petrofsky's first paralyzed test subject was Jeffrey Housh, a Wright State student who had damaged his spinal cord in a swimming pool accident in 1975. His injury was high on his spinal cord, so his paralysis was quadriplegic, affecting his arms as well as his legs.

On April 5, the researchers seated Jeff on the chair and taped a series of black, flexible electrode pads to his upper right leg. The pads were placed over the large quadriceps muscle that makes the lower leg extend. The electrode pads were wired to a computer. After the electrode pads were in place, the cuff was closed around his ankle.

Petrofsky sat at the computer. Watching Jeff carefully, he started running the program.

The computer began sending electrical impulses to the electrodes. The electrodes sent the impulses through the skin and into the muscle. As the muscle began to respond, the computer stepped up the voltage and monitored the leg for movement.

The muscle under the electrode pads quivered. Slowly, Jeff's leg—a leg that had not moved on its own in more than six years—started to straighten. His foot swung upward in a gentle kick. His leg paused, almost straight out. Then, just as gently, it settled back down.

Jeff watched silently, too amazed to say anything. He saw his leg moving, but he couldn't feel it. He knew his muscles were doing the work, but they weren't obeying his will. They were following the commands of Petrofsky's computer.

This was a milestone in Petrofsky's work. He had finally demonstrated that his method could work on humans.

This primitive system was a far cry from anything that would let a person walk away from a wheelchair.

But the person who would perform that historic feat was already on the Wright State campus.

Chapter 6

NAN

Nan Davis was a born athlete.

The second of three children and only daughter of James and Louise Davis, Nan grew up in the rural town of St. Marys, Ohio. She loved to compete in sports. She was a strong runner and set track records at St. Marys Memorial High School. She planned to run track at Ohio State University.

The St. Marys Class of 1978 graduated on the fourth of June in a festive mood. Parties were held in homes around St. Marys, and the young graduates shuttled from one to another. Nan attended one her parents were holding, another at her boyfriend's home, and a third in the nearby town of Montezuma.

The third party was slow. Friends back in St. Marys phoned to say they were confused about directions for getting to the party. It was night, and the way to Montezuma could be confusing on the dark country roads.

Nan and her boyfriend volunteered to drive back to St. Marys and guide their friends to the party. They hopped into his Volkswagen Beetle and set off into the night.

The route to St. Marys was along County Road 66A, a

winding country highway. It had a reputation for accidents; one particularly menacing turn was called Dead Man's Curve.

The Beetle zipped through Dead Man's Curve without any trouble. Nan's boyfriend reached down to push a tape into his tape player.

The next curve was closer than he realized. It caught him by surprise.

Nan looked up and saw the headlights flaring out over darkness. The road was curving away from them. She shouted, and her boyfriend hit the brakes.

But a patch of gravel lay on the asphalt surface, and the little car skidded out of control. One side tipped over the edge of the embankment. Suddenly Nan's festive evening had turned into a shattering ride in a car tumbling over and over down into a ditch.

Nan's boyfriend gripped the steering wheel. But Nan's seat came unlatched. The rolling car slammed her around inside.

Later, Nan couldn't recall the accident itself. She could only remember regaining consciousness momentarily in the wreck and realizing that she couldn't feel her legs.

Her boyfriend wasn't seriously hurt. He rushed to a nearby house and called for a rescue squad. It arrived and took Nan to the hospital in St. Marys.

Nan's parents were at home that night when a shaken

youth came to the door to report the accident. "She's not moving," he told James Davis. They went to the hospital immediately.

Nan had suffered a broken neck and a broken back. She lived, but she spent the next three months in hospitals.

Her parents could have despaired, but they refused to be gloomy. They visited Nan often. Sometimes they would take her bed down a freight elevator so she could be outside. After she was able to sit in a wheelchair, they occasionally would sneak away from the hospital with her to a fish and chips restaurant down the street.

Recovery was a slow process for Nan. Three months in the hospital was bad enough, but she had to follow that with three months of physical rehabilitation at a special center in Columbus, Ohio.

All the time, she was being told what to the best of anyone's knowledge was the absolute truth: she would never walk again. There was no cure for spinal cord injuries, the nurses and therapists told Nan, and any hope of walking someday was false hope. They urged her to forget about walking and adjust to life on wheels.

While Nan regained strength, her parents got the house ready for her homecoming. The rooms were large enough for her to move around in a wheelchair, but they had to build ramps at the doors. They added a powered chair lift to the stairway and installed handholds and rails in the bathroom.

Nan came home in a wheelchair, but she didn't sit around feeling sorry for herself. She had most of her life ahead of her, and she intended to do something with it. She enrolled at a branch campus of Wright State University near St. Marys and began studying for a degree in elementary education. She also joined the student council. Later, she moved into her own apartment near Wright State's main campus and began taking classes there.

Founded in 1964, Wright State is a relatively young university. It was designed to make attendance easy for students with physical handicaps. Underground tunnels and elevators make it possible to reach every part of the campus without having to go up or down stairs. Elevator buttons and pay phones are set low so they can be reached from wheelchairs. Such features made it easy for Nan to get around.

But Nan's spinal cord injury wasn't just a thing of the past. Paralysis involves more than not being able to move. As time went by, Nan's body changed. She could see it happening, but as far as she knew there was no way to stop it.

Nan had been used to exercising. Her leg muscles had been large and strong from years on the track team. She still got some exercise from pushing the wheels of her wheelchair, but her legs no longer moved. They were getting slimmer and, for a while, prettier. But as months of paralysis became years, her legs continued to get thinner.

What was happening to Nan happens to everyone confined to a wheelchair. She couldn't see it, but her bones also were becoming thinner and weaker. In limbs that have been paralyzed for years, Petrofsky says, "the bones can become so paper-thin they hardly show up in X-rays."

People confined to wheelchairs face serious health problems. Regular exercise is very important to keep the heart, blood vessels, and lungs healthy. But the largest muscles in the body are in the hips and legs. The exercises that do the most to keep the body healthy are those that involve the legs, such as jogging, bicycling, and cross-country skiing.

Researchers have found that people in wheelchairs suffer greatly from lack of exercise. They run a much higher risk of getting heart disease, and they are more likely to die at an early age.

The more extensive a person's paralysis, the more serious the problem is. Nan could at least use her arms for exercise. (In fact, the work of pushing herself around in a wheelchair had made her arms so strong she could beat her younger brother, John, in arm wrestling!) People with higher degrees of paralysis, such as Jeff Housh, can't even exercise their arms.

Nan wasn't aware of all these problems. But just watching her muscles shrink made her determined to find an answer. "I figured there's just got to be a way to keep your muscles up," she said later.

She joined the Spinal Cord Society to keep track of research that someday might help her. Since it was one of the organizations that funded Petrofsky's work, it printed news about his work in its newsletter.

It was in the newsletter that Nan read about Petrofsky. She was surprised to learn that he was conducting his work on the very same campus she was attending. By now it was 1982, and Petrofsky had begun his tests on people. Nan decided to volunteer as a test subject.

It wasn't that simple. Petrofsky's work was beginning to attract attention, and he was constantly in meetings or away from campus, reporting on his research at science conferences. While they shared the same campus, he might as well have been on the moon.

Nan was determined. She finally learned that he was scheduled to speak at a Spinal Cord Society conference in St. Paul, Minnesota. She drove all the way to St. Paul on June 11. Tracking him down, she found him being interviewed by a local television reporter.

Nan wheeled up to him casually and said, "It sure is something when you have to travel five hundred miles to meet someone you've been trying to meet on the same campus."

That broke the ice. She introduced herself, and Petrofsky welcomed her offer to volunteer. But he told her she would have to pass a physical examination before she could be accepted.

Chapter 7

THE ZAP MOBILE

Nan went to Petrofsky's lab for tests on June 15, 1982. "I didn't really know what to expect," she said later. A physician examined her, then laboratory assistants set her on the chair that Jeff Housh had tested in April. "They put you in the leg trainer and they test your muscle strength and your muscle endurance." (Muscle endurance is how long a muscle can work before it gets tired.) They also wanted to test the response of the motor nerves and muscles in her legs. If her paralysis involved damage to the motor nerves or to the muscles, the electrical stimulation process wouldn't work; the muscles would have lost their ability to respond.

The tests were successful. Nan was in the program.

Two days later, she rode a bike.

The lab was equipped with a stationary exercise bicycle. The front wheel—the only wheel it has—presses against a roller that can be adjusted to make the pedals harder to turn. Many people use such bikes for indoor exercise. Petrofsky was using this one to measure how much work his test subjects' legs could do and how much their fitness improved with exercise.

This exercise bike had been modified for a very unusual group of volunteers, none of whom could use their legs.

The technicians helped Nan shift from her wheelchair to the bike. It had been outfitted with a special seat and a safety belt to keep her from falling off. She wore shoes with Velcro pads on the soles that would stick to pads on the pedals. Next, they taped a series of electrode pads to each of her legs. Wires ran from the pads to a computer. They added motion sensors and more wires. Soon, Nan looked like a character from a science fiction film—only this was for real.

When everything was ready, a technician started the computer program. The computer started firing impulses to the muscles—several sets of signals to several groups of muscles. The muscles began contracting and relaxing. Nan's legs went up and down. Her feet pushed the pedals around.

She was pedaling!

She watched her legs working, exercising, bicycling for the first time in years. Suddenly all her impossible hopes seemed possible. "That was neat," Nan said later. "I loved that."

She was enjoying the chance to exercise, but she was also taking risks. She was part of an experiment.

Nobody really knew exactly what would happen when paralyzed legs were made to exercise again. Earlier experiments by other scientists had shown that electrical stimulation helped restore strength quickly in limbs of people who

had worn casts for broken bones. But some scientists thought muscles that had been paralyzed for several years would be too withered to grow strong again. One of Petrofsky's goals was to find out if this were true.

He put his test subjects through a special program of regular exercise. They rode the exercise bicycle thirty minutes per day, three days per week, to build endurance. They worked out on the leg trainer to build strength. Their progress was measured carefully during every session.

The results were dramatic. Almost immediately, Petrofsky and the others saw changes taking place. Muscle strength and endurance both increased rapidly. At the beginning, the test subjects on the average could lift only twelve pounds on the leg trainer and could bicycle only a few minutes at a rate equal to ten miles per hour. After six weeks, the average leg strength had increased to fifty-five pounds. Test subjects could pedal the bicycle at ten miles per hour for an average of thirty minutes without difficulty. Their muscles became larger. Even bones showed signs of recovering, although much more slowly than muscles.

Later, when he was presenting his findings to a group of scientists, Petrofsky said the results "surprised the tar out of us."

Nan experienced the same rapid recovery. She began going to the lab every day to ride the exercise bike or lift weights on the leg trainer.

One might think such a routine—being hoisted on and off the exercise machines, having electrodes taped to your skin, being jolted with electrical shocks—would be tiring. Maybe even painful. Not to Nan. "I'd work out three times a day if I could," she said at one point. Since her legs are paralyzed, she doesn't feel the pulses of electricity passing through her skin.

It wasn't so easy for some of the other test subjects. Jeff Housh and the other quadriplegic volunteers faced serious medical problems in exercising.

Paralysis in a quadriplegic person is like a communications blackout through most of the body. Petrofsky's process could make the legs work, but he wasn't sure how the rest of the body would respond to the effort.

When an able-bodied person exercises, the body does a number of things automatically: the lungs take in more air; the heart pumps blood faster; the sweat glands secrete moisture—perspiration—to cool the body. (Perspiration draws heat away from the skin as it evaporates.) These reflexive actions don't require orders from the brain, so signals don't have to travel to the brain to trigger a response. But paralysis can cut off communication inside the body between muscles that are exercising and the part of the nervous system that makes the body respond to exercise. The worse the paralysis, the worse the effects.

Neither paraplegic nor quadriplegic people are able to

Eleven-year-old Steve, and nine-year-old Jerry pose with their dog Missy in March, 1957.

Philip and Jeanette Petrofsky with their sons, twelve-year-old Steve and ten-year-old Jerry.

Jerry as a cub scout

Dr. Petrofsky sits at the controls of a B-17.

On November 11, 1982, newspaper and television reporters from all over the world came to Dr. Petrofsky's lab to capture the first walk Nan Davis took since her automobile accident on June 4, 1978.

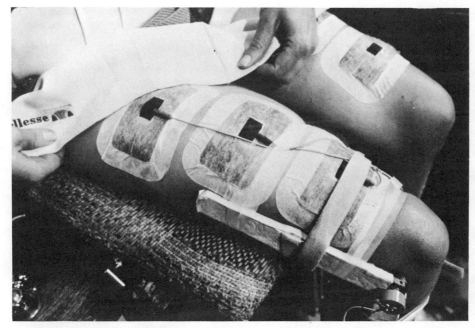

Close-up of the electrodes used to provide electrical stimulation to motor nerves in Nan's legs

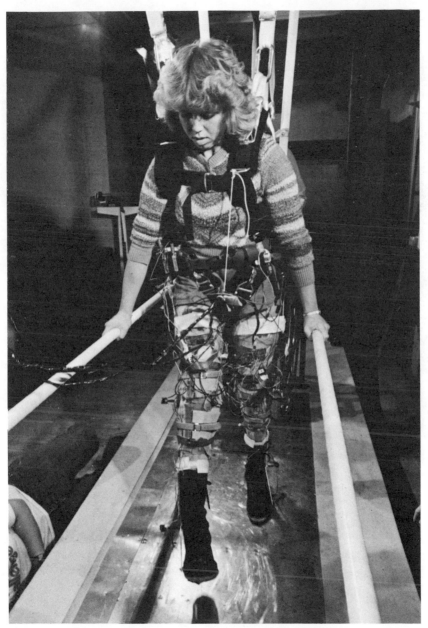

Nan, supported by a parachute harness, walks on the lab's ten-foot track. To help her keep her balance, Nan holds on to the hand rails.

The campus of Wright State University was designed to be completely accessible to handicapped students. Ramps allow wheelchair-bound students access to every part of the campus. In 1983, 450 of the university's 15,000 students had some type of physical disability.

On her birthday, November 1, 1983, Susan Steele received a phone call from President Ronald Reagan. Susan was the first quadriplegic test subject to walk and, with the aid of special devices developed by Dr. Petrofsky, use her paralyzed hands.

perspire where they are paralyzed. This was a more serious problem for quadriplegic test subjects. Since they were paralyzed over a greater part of their bodies, they would have a higher risk of overheating during exercise. Petrofsky wasn't sure whether quadriplegic test subjects doing leg exercises would perspire at all. Nor was he sure that exercise of the lower body would trigger the lungs to work harder.

Also, since quadriplegic paralysis reaches higher than the heart, Petrofsky didn't expect the hearts of quadriplegic test subjects to speed up during exercise. To meet the demand for more blood, the heart in a quadriplegic body would have to pump more blood with each beat. It was already known that quadriplegic people suffer from low blood pressure and become dizzy easily. Petrofsky worried that heavy exercise might put a strain on the hearts of quadriplegic test subjects.

Once again, the results of the tests were astonishing.

The problems Petrofsky expected did crop up at first. Jeff and other quadriplegic test subjects suffered dizziness, blood pressures became unstable, and they did not perspire where they were paralyzed. But, somehow, their bodies made adjustments. Their upper bodies broke out in heavy perspiration. They breathed hard. Their heart rates did accelerate somewhat. And blood pressure rose to a healthier level—not only during exercise, but afterward, too. Much remains to be learned about this process.

This didn't mean that everything returned to normal.

Overheating and the possibility of straining the heart were still problems. But the response was good enough to allow quadriplegics to exercise and dramatically improve their physical conditions. After several months of exercise, Jeff reported that he felt better and stronger. He said he seemed to catch cold less often. He even looked stronger.

The health benefits of the exercise have been one of the bonuses of Petrofsky's research. For the first time, people have a way to keep their paralyzed limbs strong and healthy. Petrofsky calls the technique "active physical therapy." Nan said one day that the therapeutic value of the exercise alone was reward enough for her part in the project: "If walking doesn't become feasible, if it doesn't work for some reason, I'm satisfied just to have that bike and the leg trainer just to keep my legs looking normal."

Active physical therapy is one part of Petrofsky's work that is unique. Other researchers had been experimenting with electrical stimulation or trying to find permanent cures for spinal cord injuries. But Petrofsky is the first to have developed an exercise rehabilitation program for paralyzed persons. And that will be vital preparation for anyone who intends to walk again after years of paralysis. If a miraculous cure were given to someone who had not been able to walk or exercise in years, he would be too weak to make him stand, his bones too weak to support his weight. If he did stand up, his bones would probably break.

The same thing would be true of any walking device Petrofsky developed. So, as he worked on a device to make people walk, his corps of volunteers exercised to make themselves strong enough to test it.

The research, however, was not all work and no play. There was, for example, the Zap Mobile.

During the summer of 1982, the Huffy bicycle company donated some large tricycles to Wright State. One day, looking at the quiet campus outside the laboratory windows, Petrofsky decided the weather was too nice to stay cooped up inside. He and his assistants set about customizing one of the tricycles. They made what was probably the world's first tricycle with an on-board, battery-powered computer. They modified the seat, installed a hand throttle, and added a CB radio.

With the throttle mounted on the right end of the handlebar like a motorcycle throttle, a rider could control the rate at which the computer fired the electrical impulses to make his legs move. That would control how fast the tricycle moved. It also gave the paralyzed person some control over his legs, something never before possible.

This was no ordinary vehicle. Petrofsky thought it deserved a special name. He made a big sign and mounted it on the back, behind the computer. The sign said "Zap Mobile."

In late July, the project team took the Zap Mobile

outside to the wide campus sidewalks. Nan got aboard. Technicians wired her to the computer. She twisted the throttle. And off she rode!

The throttle told the computer how fast to make Nan's muscles work and monitored the motion to keep it rhythmical. But Nan's own muscles did the work. Her legs made the Zap Mobile go.

Zap! The computer fired signals to Nan's muscles.

Zap! Nan's muscles contracted and made her legs turn the cranks.

Zap! Nan, paralyzed from the ribs down, was pedaling freely about the campus, moving under the power of her own legs for the first time in more than four years.

A small group watched Nan cruise around on the Zap Mobile. When she was done, the watchers applauded. "It was kind of embarrassing," she reported. But she enjoyed it.

The Zap Mobile was a zany project, thrown together with bits and pieces of hardware available in the lab. "The thing was probably unsafe," Petrofsky admitted later in a science conference. He noted that even the seat was made of parts scrounged up in the lab.

"The seat was wood from one of our lab drawers—we were short on wood. We didn't think anybody would notice. But when we went outside, we went past the dean and he noticed his cabinetry going by," Petrofsky said. He didn't say if their escapade upset the dean.

Chandler Phillips (left) and Jerrold Petrofsky accompany Nan Davis on the Zap Mobile.

"Zap Mobile" was a funny name, but it was an important development. It showed that a computer could make legs move in a coordinated way. It also showed that Petrofsky's process allowed paralyzed people to use their own legs to get around.

The next goal was getting Nan on her feet.

Chapter 8

WALKING

Probably because she was used to training for athletic events, Nan regained strength especially quickly. She became the prime candidate to try walking.

To develop a system to get Nan on her feet, Petrofsky's project team had to invent some things. They also had to take many components and use them in ways their inventors had never imagined.

The best example of this is the centerpiece of Petrofsky's system—the microcomputer. One of the computers he used in his early experiments, the Apple II, is used mostly for home businesses, family budgets, or video games. Petrofsky was using the Apple to help free people from their wheelchairs.

The Apple wasn't the only computer he used. As the systems became more complicated, special-purpose machines were needed. There were no computers made for what they wanted to do, so they built their own.

Before they could let Nan try to walk, Petrofsky and his colleagues had to devise elaborate safety devices to keep her from falling. If she fell, she wouldn't be able to move her legs out of the way and might break them. The computer system at that point was not sophisticated enough to catch her balance for her.

They built a large wooden framework to support a steel beam over a ten-foot track. To the beam they attached a carriage that would move back and forth along the track. The carriage supported a parachute harness. While Nan stood, a thirty-pound barbell attached to the harness as a counterweight would help keep part of her weight off her joints and bones. If she fell, the harness would catch her before she hit the floor. To help her keep her balance, they bordered the track with a pair of handrails.

In August, 1982, just two months after she had first wheeled herself into Petrofsky's lab, Nan stood up.

Later, she didn't recall having an emotional reaction to the event. "I'm a nonreactive person," she said with a laugh. But she added that another volunteer, after standing for the first time in Petrofsky's experimental harness, went into a rest room and cried.

By November, Petrofsky was ready for Nan to try to walk. The prospect of such an event was drawing more and more interest.

The CBS television program "60 Minutes" featured Petrofsky on the first Sunday in November. It broke the news to millions of viewers that he would try to make Nan walk the following week.

The next day, the response hit Wright State like a tidal wave.

Newspapers, magazines, and TV networks from around the world started calling the university. Everybody wanted to send reporters to cover the event. Wright State's phone lines were swamped. Nobody could call out of Petrofsky's lab. The university scrambled to order five more phone lines for Petrofsky's office. Petrofsky had a line with an unlisted number put in the lab. Carol Siyahi, a university press representative who had been handling questions about Petrofsky's work, spent the whole day answering a flood of calls from reporters.

The university scheduled a press conference and a demonstration for November 11. But Nan had not yet proved that the system would work. Her paralyzed legs had not yet taken their first steps.

They spent long hours in the lab, working a twenty-four-hour schedule, locked away from the curious media. They worked until they were exhausted and took catnaps on the floor. They phoned out for pizzas when they got hungry.

On the night before the press conference Nan finally walked in the harness. But the big test would come the next morning, when the eyes of the world would be watching Nan to see whether she walked—or not.

The press conference was a turbulent affair. Reporters and photographers from the United States, Brazil, England, France, and West Germany crowded into the building where the biomedical labs were located. The university's press representatives offered sandwiches and coffee downstairs and posted security guards outside the doors to the lab upstairs. Siyahi found herself trying to be in both places at once.

But newspeople like to go where the news is. They like to find out things no other reporters have found out. One by one or in pairs, reporters and photographers would wander upstairs and try to get into the lab.

Most of them were turned away, but one network television crew got inside. They immediately started setting up their equipment. In all the confusion, the people in the lab thought the crew was supposed to be there. The sound man asked Petrofsky if he would wear a "bug"—a hidden, wireless microphone that would transmit everything he said. Petrofsky, an affable man and a nut about anything electronic, agreed.

But the camera operator caused trouble. His bright, hot floodlight came too close to the delicate sensory harness and melted some of the wiring. Petrofsky's assistants made some quick repairs. He said later that the accident came close to ruining the demonstration.

Outside the lab, another television crew knew the network crew was inside. They were angry; they wanted in, too. They voiced their complaint when Siyahi came by. Instead of letting another crew in, she went into the lab and ordered the network crew to leave.

A little bit later, Petrofsky told her about the accident with the sensory harness and said there was a chance the demonstration wouldn't work. Already run ragged by the press, "I just about went through the roof," Siyahi said later. She made several choice remarks to Petrofsky about the crew and its meddling.

She had no way of knowing that Petrofsky was still wearing the network crew's bug. Petrofsky kept a straight face and said nothing. The very people she was lambasting heard every word. After the day's events were over and the pressure was off, the network crew teased Siyahi about what they had overheard. Her face turned red, but she was able to laugh with them.

Through it all, Nan sat patiently in her wheelchair while the lab technicians taped and wired and strapped her legs. She didn't seem to mind that the doorway was jammed with reporters craning their necks to see her. Later she would tell a reporter she was just too tired to be nervous.

There were far too many reporters and photographers to fit into the lab with the project team. Expecting this to be the case, the university had set up a closed-circuit TV system. Press, radio, and TV reporters crowded into a room next to the lab, where they could watch everything on TV monitors. TV camera crews hooked up their equipment to the closed-circuit system so they could record what the university's TV camera picked up. The closed-circuit system gave everybody a view of the event without overcrowding the lab. Only newspaper and magazine photographers, who had to be in the same room with Nan to shoot their pictures, were allowed inside the lab.

Nan was ready. She maneuvered her wheelchair through the lab and got into position at the end of the track. She put on the safety harness. Petrofsky stationed himself at the computer console, one eye on a bank of warning lights. He turned on the system and started the computer.

Nan stood up—but she didn't go anywhere. Something was out of adjustment. She sat back down.

Again she stood up—and again. Each time, something needed to be adjusted. After several attempts, Petrofsky ordered a rest break for Nan. Standing up time after time was tiring her leg muscles.

Reporters worried about meeting their deadlines. TV crews hoped they wouldn't run out of videotape. And everyone wondered the same thing. Would it work?

Finally, everything seemed ready. Petrofsky powered up the system. Nan stood. Petrofsky ordered the computer to begin the walking sequences. Nan's right leg rose and moved forward.

Again and again her wired legs bent, swung forward, straightened. Nan walked to the end of the track and

Petrofsky shut down the system. Nan sat back in her wheel-chair. Everybody broke out in applause. Nan had just made history.

More than a few people who watched the walk were reminded of an earlier historic step—Astronaut Neil Armstrong's first step onto the moon in 1969. "That's one small step for a man, one giant leap for mankind," he had said. When Nan finished her walk, and everyone was asking her for a comment, she quipped: "That's one small step for a woman, one giant leap for womankind." The *Cincinnati Enquirer* went her one better. The headline on its story proclaimed "One Small Step for Nan."

Nan had taken some very important steps, but they were just the first. This was only the beginning of what Petrofsky wanted to do. And there were others like Nan who were trying desperately to walk.

Chapter 9

SUSAN

On the evening of August 25, 1979, sixteen-year-old Susan Steele was riding with some friends to a football game in Alexandria, Virginia. It was a rainy evening. The roads were slick. The car slid through a turn and into a ditch.

It wasn't a serious accident, Susan said later. They should have been able to walk away and call a tow truck. But in some manner that she doesn't recall, Susan hit her neck against something.

She couldn't walk away from the accident. She couldn't walk at all. She had injured her spinal cord. In an instant, a high school student who loved to swim and play soccer was paralyzed from the chest down. Even her hands could make only the faintest of motions. Susan, a tall girl who had stood five-feet eleven-inches, had to look up at everyone from her wheelchair.

Like Nan, Susan was told to accept her condition. There was no cure for spinal cord injuries, no reason to hope.

She went on with life, enrolling in college, but that no-hope advice angered her. She didn't believe in accepting things without trying to change them. She heard about research being done to find a cure for spinal cord injuries, and she refused to believe that nobody would find an answer. "I always knew there would be a solution," she said later, "but I never thought it would be through a computer."

She learned about Petrofsky's work three years after her accident. She heard about it from her older sister, Cindy, who worked for the American Paralysis Association. Petrofsky was working with human test subjects by then. Excited, Susan called Petrofsky long-distance to volunteer as a test subject. He asked her to send copies of her medical records and invited her to Wright State for testing. In August, 1982—about the time Nan was pedaling around campus on the Zap Mobile—Susan Steele transferred to Wright State and joined Petrofsky's project.

She started out with the standard exercises—regular workouts on the leg trainer and the stationary exercise bicycle. "The first time I rode the bike, it was really exciting because once again my whole body was moving," she said later. "I felt real athletic."

She began to notice changes. She started feeling better. Stronger. Her legs, which had grown spindly from years of paralysis, began to look healthier. "I've noticed a great deal of change in my legs," she reported after six months in the program. "They look healthier. They're not just dead limbs."

Her improvement was so rapid that Petrofsky put her in training for the walking harness. Because walking would be much harder for quadriplegics than for paraplegics, Susan

Steele and Jeff Housh were the only two quadriplegics being trained to walk.

Standing for the first time in three years was a strange experience for her. Under computer control, her legs pushed her up out of the chair. The harness supported part of her weight. "It was strange to have people looking up at me again," she recalled. "In a way, all of a sudden it felt normal. It felt like it should be that way."

She took her first steps on April 25, 1983, five months after Nan's headline-making walk. This time, the university wanted to avoid another mob scene with newspeople. It made no advance announcement of the attempt.

Susan was nervous. It had worked for Nan. What if it didn't work for her? Could she really walk after three and a half years of paralysis?

She could and did. "It was overwhelming," she said later. "You forget what it's like."

But walking wasn't all Petrofsky had in mind for Susan. He had been continuing to work with Nan, improving the system, and doing research in other areas.

One area was the walking itself. He referred to Nan's first walks as "ambulation," because they lacked the smoothness and coordination of normal walking. He increased the number of muscles stimulated by the computer, which made the whole system much more complex. He also added four sensors not much larger than pencil erasers to give the computer control of balance. The tiny devices, called level detectors, worked like gyroscopes. They had been designed for air-to-air missiles, but Petrofsky found them perfect for his work. With level detectors in the system, the computer could tell if someone was starting to fall and make the legs move to catch his or her balance.

Another area is what Petrofsky calls "voluntary control." Voluntary control gives a person control of paralyzed muscles. Instead of doing whatever the computer is programmed to do, a person with voluntary control can make the computer do what he or she wants.

Petrofsky used new sensors for the voluntary control harness. Made of a stretchable woven material, they were much more flexible than anything he had used before. He had them sewn into the shoulders of test subjects' clothing. When Nan or Susan wanted to walk forward, she moved her shoulders forward. The motion would send signals to the computer, which would stimulate her muscles to walk forward. When she wanted to walk backward, she moved her shoulders back, and the computer would send her stepping backward.

Another system Petrofsky designed had nothing to do with walking. It was a small computer-controlled system that would allow a person to use paralyzed hands. He wanted Susan to try it.

Susan has close to normal movement in her arms. "What I

don't have is my fingers. If I was injured any higher up, I would have lost [the use of] my arms," she said. The hand controller worked by stimulating muscles in a forearm. It could either bend her fingers into a fist or straighten them. With a control harness, she could make her hand grasp things by hunching her shoulders.

In the lab, she practiced picking up a beaker full of water, moving it around, and setting it back down without spilling it. She also practiced holding a hairbrush and brushing her hair with it. "It was fascinating because I hadn't been able to get a good grip like that," she said later. She had been using combs with special handles she could hold with an open hand. The hand controller needed much more development before it would allow Susan to control each individual finger—but Susan had experienced enough already to convince her that in time it would happen.

Chapter 10

WINGS

Nan's first walk had made worldwide news. The publicity made both Nan and Petrofsky celebrities. It seemed everyone wanted to meet or talk to them. They were invited to appear on TV talk shows. Magazines wanted to feature them. Letters poured into Petrofsky's office, sometimes at the rate of more than two hundred a day. Petrofsky found himself the center of attention everywhere he went.

All the attention was a mixed blessing. Petrofsky thought it showed that more people were becoming concerned about research aimed at helping people in wheelchairs—people who, in Petrofsky's opinion, are all but ignored by society. On the other hand, the demands on his time became overwhelming. His staff had to lock the laboratory door to keep out curious reporters. He found himself spending less and less time on his research as he flew from one part of the country to another to deliver speeches, appear at science conferences, or testify before Congress on the need for more funds for spinal cord research.

Somehow, though, he always found a way to squeeze in extra activities. Just as in childhood, Petrofsky seemed to be in the midst of a whirlwind of activity, involved in so many pursuits at once that nobody was ever quite sure what he would be doing from one day to the next.

If there is any one place that reflects this aspect of Petrofsky's nature, it may be the basement of his home in Beavercreek, Ohio. Furnished with bright red carpeting and black vinyl furniture, the room is a mad combination of family room, hobby center, and penny arcade.

What is true of Petrofsky's basement one day may not be true the next. But on one particular day, Petrofsky had installed two full-size video arcade games along the wall to the right of the stairs. One was an electronic shooting gallery; the other was a dot-eating maze game similar to Pac-Man. On the other side of the stairs was a small room that was Petrofsky's radio shack. It was filled with radio transmitters, computers, and other equipment.

The main family room was oriented around a console TV set. But it was obvious that the Petrofsky family does more with its TV than watch soap operas. On the set sat a video tape recorder and a home computer. A long shelf on the wall was filled with videotapes.

At the other end of the room stood two crank-operated arcade machines. Sometimes Petrofsky jokes about having an extra room built on his house for an arcade.

But his favorite pastime, one that has lasted since childhood, seems to be flying. Petrofsky owns or is part owner of three planes: a small, single-engine Cessna 172; a twin-engine (and something of a classic) Cessna 310; and a re-stored T-6, a World War II combat trainer.

"I first got interested in World War II aircraft when I was about five or six years old," Petrofsky said one day. (He was flying in a commercial jetliner at the time.) "St. Louis used to have a big fair down by the river front once a year in the area where the [Gateway] Arch is now. When I was five or six years old, I remember, they had a B-29 down there, and I went through the thing. It was just the fuselage—they didn't have the wings on it. They had trucked it in. I really got interested in it at that point."

Petrofsky had his first airplane flight in a Cessna 172, a small four-seater, single-engine plane. He flew in it from his college campus in Rolla, Missouri, to St. Louis. "It kinda scared me. The guy flew for a new airline that went out of business after about half a year. He had retired as a pilot with the Blue Angels [the Navy stunt-flying team]. We went over Sullivan, Missouri. I was looking down and I said, 'Gee, is that Sullivan?' He said, 'Let's take a look'—and he did a barrel roll."

Petrofsky started taking flying lessons twice in college, but both times he had to stop when he ran out of money. He resumed them several years later when his move from St. Louis to Dayton left him with a month of free time. But a busy schedule made him put them off once more.

Finally, in 1981, "I decided either I was going to learn how

to fly or not learn how to fly. I had to force myself to do it."
He signed up for an aviation course at Wright State. He got
his pilot's license and bought the 172 he had learned to fly in.
"Then I thought, 'Gee, now I know how to fly; I can go wherever I want.' I put my family in the plane and headed down
to Florida."

He quickly learned that flying is not so simple.

He landed in Chattanooga, Tennessee, then took off again.
"I ran right into storms and severe turbulence, diverted to
Atlanta, got a rent-a-car and drove down to Florida. . . .I
began to realize there was a great deal of virtue in getting
an instrument rating, because it was rather obvious that
private pilots can kill themselves."

After that he went back to ground school and learned how
to fly in bad weather, using only the plane's instruments for
guidance. He also decided to get a commercial pilot's rating
and, when he found the Cessna 310 for sale, he earned a
rating for flying multi-engine aircraft. In the spirit of the
Zap Mobile, he named his new plane the *Aerozap One*.

He flies mostly on business trips, he said. It's fun and it
saves time. With his own plane he doesn't have to worry
about airline schedules.

Petrofsky also likes to fly for sheer pleasure. But for that,
something as tame as a 172 or even a 310 just wouldn't do.
Petrofsky wanted something with power, prestige, and history to it. He wanted a warbird.

It was Petrofsky's multi-engine flight instructor, Russell Cook, who rekindled his old interest in World War II planes. Cook is a member of the Confederate Air Force, a national organization of aviation buffs who restore and fly World War II airplanes. In fact, Cook was safety officer for the Ohio Valley Squadron (now Wing) of the CAF. Cook talked to Petrofsky about the organization, and Petrofsky decided to join.

It was a mutual exchange of interests. Cook became fascinated by Petrofsky's research and went to work for him as a lab technician.

Together they looked for a plane of their own. World War II aircraft are rare and expensive. Although thousands of fighters and bombers were built during the war, most were scrapped afterward. Now the more famous combat planes cost hundreds of thousands of dollars.

What still exists in relatively large numbers is the T-6 Texan, a single-engine plane that was used to train combat pilots. T-6s survived because the United States sold many to foreign countries for use as combat planes in their air forces.

Eventually Petrofsky and Cook learned of someone who had bought a number of T-6s from Spain. Some had spent the decades since World War II in their original crates— never even assembled until recently. Petrofsky and Cook ended up buying a nearly forty-year-old plane in like-new

condition. Only rubber parts that had turned brittle over the years had to be replaced, and some new instruments and radios were added. When they finally got it to Dayton and parked it among its civilian, modern-age brethren, it looked like a ghost from the past—a silver ghost with Spanish air force markings.

One of Petrofsky's most memorable flights, however, was in a real classic of World War II—a B-17 Flying Fortress.

The B-17 is one of the most famous planes in the world. Bristling with machine guns, the four-engine bomber flew by the thousands over Germany during World War II. It has been the star of movies and books. *Twelve O'Clock High* was a movie about the B-17 that later became a TV series.

But very few B-17s survive, and only a few outfitted as bombers still fly. Two are owned by the Confederate Air Force. It was through the CAF that Petrofsky got the chance to take a five-hundred-mile flight in the B-17 *Texas Raiders*.

The CAF doesn't let just anyone fly one of its planes. A chance to fly in the *Texas Raiders* was unusual even for a CAF member. But the offer was extended to Petrofsky in recognition of his work to help the handicapped.

On June 22, 1983, he and Cook flew in a jetliner to Newark, New Jersey, and had a friend drive them to Morristown. They found the *Texas Raiders* standing by itself at the airport. The pilots arrived and opened the plane. They climbed inside and found it oven-hot. The metal bomber had been sitting in the sun all morning, soaking up its rays.

They took off with engines roaring and sailed into the clouds over New Jersey and Pennsylvania. The wind and altitude cooled the plane quickly. For four hours Petrofsky and Cook took turns exploring the plane and sitting in the pilot's seat, handling the controls but trying nothing fancy. The bomber was thirty-nine years old, but the B-17 had a reputation for reliability. It plied the skyways without a shudder, crossing Ohio and landing at an air show in Mount Comfort, Indiana.

Petrofsky seems happily addicted to the old warbirds. He and Cook even flew their 600-horsepower T-6 at the Dayton International Air Show, zooming past the crowds at almost two hundred miles an hour just a few feet off the ground.

Petrofsky flew for fun quite a bit during the summer of 1983. Before that, he didn't have time. The winter and spring of 1983 were one of the busiest periods of his life.

Work in the lab was picking up speed. They were striving to meet an important deadline for a special project—Nan's graduation.

The last time Nan had walked outside a laboratory had been on her high school graduation day. On June 11, graduation day at Wright State, it would be exactly five years since that last walk. When she went forward to receive her diploma, she wanted to do it on her feet.

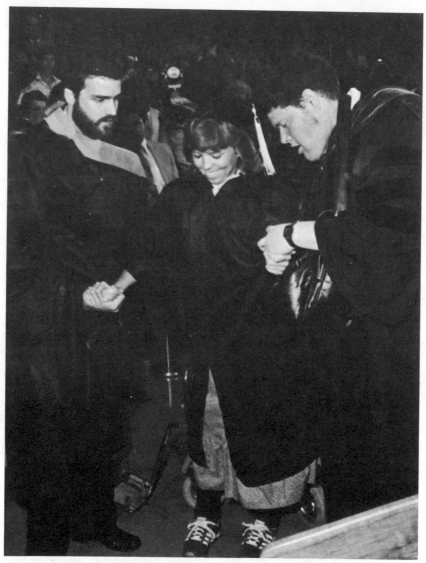

Holding the hands of Dr. Petrofsky and research assistant, Don Stafford (left), Nan Davis walked to receive her bachelor's degree on June 11, 1983. The portable computer system, which controls the movements of Nan's legs, is in the bag under Dr. Petrofsky's arm.

Chapter 11

GRADUATION

The work in Petrofsky's lab now focused on an important new phase of the walking project. It was a portable, battery-powered system, no bigger than a book, that would allow a paralyzed person to walk outside the laboratory.

When Petrofsky first began studying physiology, computers were all huge machines the size of refrigerators, like the LINC. If he had developed his walking process then, it would have had no practical value. A person would have needed a truck to follow him around, part of it containing the computer, part containing a portable power plant.

Microcomputers changed all that. With the technology of the early 1980s, Petrofsky could shrink his system down to a point where walking would be practical. The system he was developing would run on a battery pack. The computer itself would be able to fit inside a purse. Only the wires running to electrodes and sensors would show. And even they could be hidden.

By late winter, Nan no longer needed the parachute harness. Her bones had grown strong enough to support her weight. When she walked she stood upright. The computer kept her balanced with the aid of tiny level detectors.

In fact, Nan was now able to walk without holding on to the handrail. She began practicing with a pair of canes instead. She began wearing long, full skirts in the lab to see how well they concealed the electrodes and wires and straps on her legs. All the hardware stayed out of sight except for the wires going to the computer. With the computer close to her, tucked under her arm in a handbag, for example, even the wires were inconspicuous. The system could let Nan fulfill her wish of walking to receive her degree.

But June was approaching, and the system was proving difficult to develop. Not only did Petrofsky's team have to design a new computer system, but they also had to rewrite all the walking instructions to work with the new electronics. They also had to make the whole package of instructions— the program—small enough to fit into the computer's small memory. Petrofsky put the lab on a night-shift schedule to avoid interruptions. Researchers and test subjects came in late in the day and worked all night.

Finally, it was the last week before graduation. The work still wasn't finished. Everybody worked harder. This was no longer just research. It was for Nan.

On Thursday morning, June 9, 1983, the team went into the lab. They stayed through Thursday night and came out briefly on Friday afternoon. Everyone went home for short naps, then returned about 8:00 P.M. and stayed behind the locked doors until 2:00 A.M. Saturday. It was graduation day.

Wright State didn't have a hall large enough for graduation ceremonies, so it rented the University of Dayton's sports arena. That Saturday morning at the arena, another crowd of reporters and photographers was on hand, mingling with more than a thousand students and professors clad in black caps and gowns.

A large platform had been erected at the front of the arena. Dr. Robert J. Kegerreis, president of the university, and other college officials shared the platform with students who were to receive special honors. The floor of the arena was filled with folding chairs for the graduating students. On all sides rose the arena seats, where families and friends of the graduates were sitting.

On the floor next to the platform stood a lecture podium. Facing it was a row of reserved chairs. A gap just wide enough for a wheelchair was left in the middle of the row. But neither Nan nor Petrofsky was anywhere in sight.

The graduation ceremonies took place as usual. More than eight thousand people watched the graduates go forward to receive their diplomas. At last, all the diplomas had been handed out. All but one.

A collective gasp arose from the crowd. A small procession of robed people was coming in the front right entrance, followed by a pack of photographers. At once, everybody recognized the young blond woman seated in the chrome wheelchair. She was just another graduating student, but she was also famous. Everybody there had heard of her, and undoubtedly most had seen her on television. Petrofsky, Phillips, and several assistants accompanied her, all dressed in black caps and gowns and stifling occasional yawns.

No computer system was in sight. However, people standing close to Nan might have noticed a very odd, bulky bracelet on her left wrist. They might also have noticed a bundle of wires emerging from a camera bag on her lap and disappearing into her gown. The bracelet contained a small display of lights that would allow Petrofsky to monitor the computer system by standing next to Nan and holding her arm. The computer system and battery pack were tucked inside the bag. Hidden under her black gown were the harnesses of sensors and electrodes on her legs. Nearby, research associate Harry Heaton III stood ready for emergencies. He was wearing a small electronics repair kit in a vest under his own gown.

Dr. Kegerreis read a proclamation from the governor of Ohio that praised Petrofsky for his "research genius" and Nan for her "unceasing will." Then he began reading a letter that had been written to Nan. In part it said:

I know this day is uniquely special for you, Nan, as things have not been easy. But your determination and courage have persevered, and we all are proud of you. Life is full of struggles for many of us, but you are a fighter and can achieve whatever you desire.

The letter, Kegerreis announced, was signed by Ronald Reagan, president of the United States.

Then, addressing Nan directly, he told her to "come forward and receive your degree."

Petrofsky and an assistant, doctoral student Donald Stafford, maneuvered Nan's wheelchair to a spot where she had a clear path to the podium. Then, with one of the men on each side of her, Nan stood up. Applause filled the arena.

Photographers surrounded her. Every photographer wanted a clear shot of Nan's walk, but they blocked everybody else's view. There was barely a pathway for Nan to walk.

She stepped forward. There was no parachute harness this time. No black paratrooper boots. She was wearing blue sneakers, and she had only Petrofsky and Stafford on each arm for balance. Petrofsky held the bag with the computer in it and hunched over Nan's arm as she walked forward. His eyes darted between the little display of lights on her wrist and the floor in front of her.

Nan took several shuffling steps to the platform, her legs hidden under the gown. Because the photographers managed to get in one another's way, only a few cameras that day captured her feet taking one step after another.

The plan had been for Nan to walk past the podium, receive her diploma from the dean of the college of education, then turn back to the podium and face the audience.

Instead, Petrofsky said later, when she came alongside the podium she turned and made an instinctive grab for it. The sudden twisting motion pulled an electrode loose from one leg, and the leg went limp under her.

Petrofsky and Stafford supported Nan and moved her the last foot or two to the podium. She held on to it while the computer drove the muscles in her other leg as hard as they would go to keep her upright. In moments she was gasping from the exertion.

But she didn't stop smiling. Speaking into a microphone, she told her fellow graduates:

> This is a special day for all of us. Everyone of us who is graduating has worked hard for this moment. What makes it more special for me is the fact that this is the first time I've walked outside of Dr. Petrofsky's lab since I graduated from high school—thank you Dr. Petrofsky.
>
> I know that a lot of attention had been paid to me for my participation in Dr. Petrofsky's research project. But all of us have had our triumphs and setbacks over the years. We have all worked hard to be where we are today, and I would like to congratulate you all.

Chapter 12

THE NEXT STEPS

Jerrold Petrofsky has shown that paralyzed people can walk again—not just in the lab, but out in public. Even more important, he has shown that people paralyzed for years can be brought back to health with the aid of computer-controlled electrical stimulation. Petrofsky's work is full of promise, but the promise must be kept. To help the thousands who need it, the research must be brought out of the lab and put into products for the public.

That's happening now.

On December 21, 1982, a company was formed to develop commercial versions of the electrical stimulation systems in Petrofsky's lab. The company's name is Therapeutic Technologies, Inc.

The man who launched TTI is Martin Ergas, an attorney in Miami, Florida. He is also a victim of a spinal cord injury and more than casually interested in Jerrold Petrofsky's work.

A member of the American Paralysis Association, Ergas met Jerrold Petrofsky in September, 1981, at a scientific conference sponsored by the association. "Of all the people speaking, I understood what Petrofsky was saying," Ergas

Nan Davis and Jerrold Petrofsky

said later. And what Petrofsky was saying—that paralyzed muscles could be made useful again—fascinated him.

After Nan's walk in November, 1982, Ergas brought together several people as investors, incorporated the company under the laws of the state of Florida, and began negotiating with Wright State for licenses to make and sell Petrofsky's devices. (Since Petrofsky works for the university, the university controls the patent rights.)

TTI's directors decided the company's engineering staff and assembly plant should be located near Wright State. That would make it easier to consult with Petrofsky and his associates when problems arose. They rented an office in Xenia, Ohio, not far from the university, and on April 11, 1983, hired a general manager to run operations there. The manager's name? Steven Petrofsky.

While Jerrold Petrofsky had pursued his Ph.D. and his electrical stimulation research, his brother had pursued his own career as an electrical engineer. He designed state-of-the-art microelectronic devices for Emerson Electric Company and did consulting work on his own. But, over the years, he had stayed in touch with his brother and had helped him develop the computer control system for electrical stimulation. When TTI tapped him to run its operations, he was already familiar with the work.

TTI's first products are to be exercise devices for use in hospitals or other clinical settings under medical supervision.

It will be the first time that people have a chance to exercise paralyzed limbs—not just have them moved to keep joints limber, but actually make the muscles work, helping bone recovery and blood circulation as well. These first products will not put paralyzed people back on their feet, but they will help them prepare for the day when that might become possible.

Jerrold Petrofsky continues to work toward that goal. In January, 1983, the university promoted him to full professor and named him first executive director of its new National Center for Rehabilitation Engineering.

By the autumn of 1983, he had developed an even smaller version of the portable walking system Nan had used at graduation. "It's a much better system," he said. He's using it to develop an even smaller system, one the size of a postage stamp. The system he envisions will be reduced to a single microprocessor chip containing all the instructions needed to control and monitor muscles and movement. A system that small, battery operated and completely out of sight, could be implanted inside a person's body by a surgeon. As this book went to press, Petrofsky estimated he was within a year of having an experimental version ready for testing.

It will be several years before such a system is available to the public. Exhaustive tests must be conducted to make sure it's foolproof. There must be no little, undiscovered quirks in the system that could cause a person to fall or go stomping out of control. (A quirk that suddenly sent someone walking into traffic, or trying to walk up steps on a stairway going down, could be fatal.) It must also be easy to use, allowing a person to stand, walk, and sit without constantly thinking about it. As with any medical device that is surgically implanted, the walking system will have to meet the approval of the United States Food and Drug Administration. The FDA is responsible for making sure new medical inventions are safe, and its review process usually takes years.

For Nan, Susan, and the other test subjects who have walked again, it will be years of impatient waiting. It will not be idle waiting, however. They continue to work with Petrofsky, exercising daily and testing the latest refinements in the walking system.

Every step they take is a step toward the future. And every step is a step for thousands of others who are waiting.

JERROLD PETROFSKY

Jerrold Scott Petrofsky was born on May 5, 1948, in St. Louis, Missouri. He earned a Ph.D. degree in physiology from the St. Louis University Medical School in 1974. He completed postdoctoral research there in 1976 and joined its faculty as an assistant professor of physiology.

He joined the Wright State University faculty as associate professor of biomedical engineering in 1979. In January, 1983, he was named professor and was appointed the first executive director of the National Center for Rehabilitation Engineering.

He has received numerous awards, including the Dayton Section, Institute for Electrical and Electronic Engineers' (IEEE) Noble Award for Engineering, 1981; the IEEE's "Special Award" for continuing outstanding work, 1983; the ADD (Abilities Demonstrated by the Disabled) Research Project of the Year Award, 1982; the American Paralysis Association's and the Spinal Cord Society's Scientist of the Year awards, 1982; the State of Ohio Governor's Award, 1983; and a resolution citing outstanding achievement from the Ohio General Assembly, 1983, among others.

He has published many scholarly papers and several

Jerrold Petrofsky and a B-17 called "Texas Raiders"

books and holds a number of patents. He is a member of numerous professional societies.

He lives in Beavercreek, Ohio, with his wife, Cheryl, and his daughter, Melissa, and son, David Andrew.

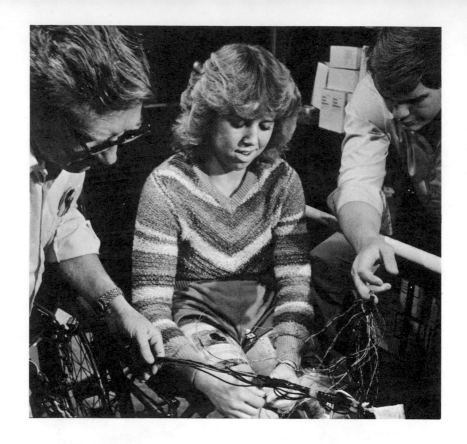

NANETTE DAVIS

Nanette Louise Davis was born on April 15, 1960. She graduated cum laude with a bachelor's degree in elementary education from Wright State University in June, 1983. She was injured in an automobile accident on June 4, 1978. A test subject for Dr. Jerrold Petrofsky since June 15, 1982, she was the first person with paralyzed legs to pedal a modified tricycle and the first to walk with the aid of computerized electrical stimulation. She is from St. Marys, Ohio.

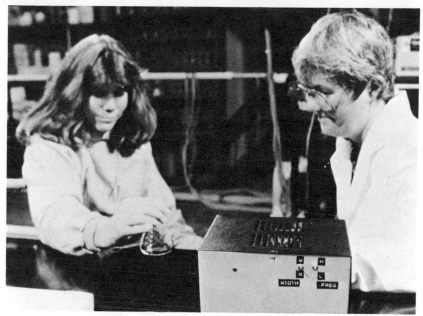

Susan Steele demonstrates a hand-control system in the lab.

SUSAN STEELE

Susan Elaine Steele was born on November 1, 1962. She was injured in an automobile accident on August 25, 1979. A communications and political science major at Wright State University, she joined Dr. Petrofsky's research efforts in August, 1982. She was the first quadriplegic test subject to walk and use paralyzed hands with the aid of Dr. Petrofsky's devices. She is from Alexandria, Virginia.

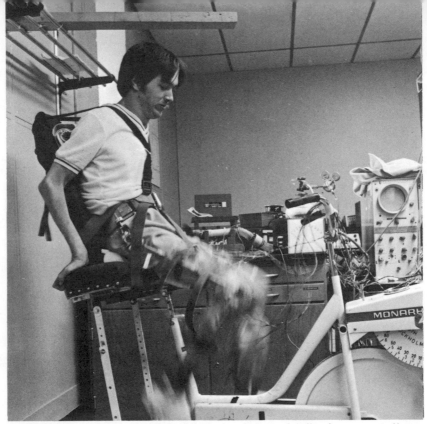

Assisted by a computerized electrical stimulation - feedback system, Jeffrey Housh pedals the lab's stationary bicycle.

JEFFREY HOUSH

Jeffrey S. Housh was born on May 2, 1959. He was injured in a swimming accident on June 30, 1975. As a junior majoring in political science at Wright State University, he was the first paralyzed person to try Dr. Petrofsky's process. He is from Middletown, Ohio.

LUIGI GALVANI

Luigi Galvani was born on September 9, 1737, in Bologna, Italy. He attended the University of Bologna, obtained a medical degree there, and lectured on anatomy.

His early research was in comparative anatomy. He began lecturing on electrophysiology in the 1770s. With an electrostatic machine to generate electricity and a Leyden jar (an early form of battery) to store it, he began to experiment with electrical stimulation of muscles. From the 1780s on, this became his major field of study.

He published his findings in 1791. He believed the brain secreted an "electric fluid" that differed from natural or artificially generated electricity. He demonstrated his theory that electricity in the body controlled muscular movement by opening the spinal cord of a frog and connecting it by way of a metal rod to one of the frog's legs. When the rod touched the leg, the muscle contracted.

His findings were generally accepted, but they were challenged by Alessandro Volta, professor of physics at the University of Pavia in Italy. Volta believed the muscle was responding to electrical action generated in the rod by the presence of two different metals.

Both men were partly right. Later, Galvani proved his theory by inducing muscle contraction by touching the nerve of one frog to the muscle of another, causing contraction without the use of any metal. Galvani's work contributed to Volta's discovery of the voltaic pile, or battery. Galvani died at age sixty-one on December 4, 1798.

WRIGHT STATE UNIVERSITY

Located near Dayton, Ohio, Wright State University was designed to be completely accessible to handicapped students. About 450 of Wright State's 15,000 students have some physical disability. Many of them are confined to wheelchairs.

The university administration includes an office of handicapped student services that oversees a wide variety of special services. They include housing built to be accessible to people in wheelchairs, attendant care, transportation, and athletic programs designed for people with physical disabilities.

Wright State is a center for a number of research efforts directed at helping the physically handicapped. In January, 1983, the university established the National Center for Rehabilitation Engineering and began planning new research facilities.

A NOTE ABOUT COMPUTERS

The "brain" of every microcomputer is a microprocessor, a tiny electronic chip that does the actual computing. This book was written on a KayPro II microcomputer. Its microprocessor, a Zilog Z80, is the same kind of chip that enabled Nan Davis to walk.

ABOUT THE AUTHOR

Timothy R. Gaffney is a staff feature writer for the *Dayton Daily News* and the *Journal Herald*, publications of Dayton Newspapers, Inc. He began reporting on Dr. Petrofsky's work in January, 1981, and has followed his research since then. His first story on Dr. Petrofsky won third place in the National Society of Professional Engineers' 1982 newspaper and magazine journalism contest. He has won state awards for feature writing from the Ohio Associated Press, the Ohio Newspaper Women's Association, and the Ohio Public Images Association. He lives in Miamisburg, Ohio, with his wife, Jean, and his daughter, Kimberly.

Jerrold Petrofsky 1948-

1948 Jerrold Petrofsky is born in St. Louis. The transistor is invented. Organization of American States founded. Czechoslovakia and Hungary taken over by Communist party. Berlin airlift. (Supplies are flown into West Berlin when Soviets blockade city.) State of Israel is born; Arabs attack it. Gandhi is assassinated.

1949 Breeder reactor developed by Atomic Energy Commission; it makes more fuel than it uses. Soviet Union develops the atomic bomb. George Orwell publishes *1984*. End of Chinese civil war. People's Republic of China is created.

1950 Senator Joseph McCarthy charges that there are Communists in the State Department.

1951 The first mass-produced computer (UNIVAC I) makes debut. Julius and Ethel Rosenberg are convicted of conspiring to pass military secrets to Russians. Churchill becomes prime minister again.

1952 Dwight Eisenhower elected president of the United States. King George VI of England dies; his daughter Elizabeth becomes queen. MauMau revolt against British rule in Kenya.

1953 U.S. gives financial aid to France to help her repel rebels in Vietnam. Death of Stalin; Georgi Malenkov becomes premier of Soviet Union. Basic structure of DNA determined by James Watson and Francis Crick.

1954 U.S. Supreme Court rules that segregation in public schools is unconstitutional. Jonas Salk develops injectable vaccine for polio. French defeated in Vietnam.

1955 U.S. begins to send aid to South Vietnam, Laos and Cambodia. Dr. Martin Luther King leads boycott of segregated buses in Montgomery, Alabama. Albert Sabin develops oral vaccine for polio. Revolution overthrows Juan Peron in Argentina. Israel attacked by three neighboring countries.

1956 President Eisenhower is reelected. Anti-Communist rebellion put down in Hungary.

1957 Governor of Arkansas tries to prevent integration at Central High School in Little Rock. Federal troops enforce Supreme Court ruling. Sputnik I & II, the first artificial satellites, are launched by Soviet Union. U.N. forces sent to Israeli border areas to keep peace.

1958 NASA (National Aeronautics and Space Administration) is set up. Explorer I, America's first satellite, is sent into space. Charles DeGaulle becomes French president. Revolt in Algeria against French.

1959 Space program launches a number of historic missions. Fidel Castro comes to power in Cuba.

1960 John F. Kennedy elected president. Theodore Maiman develops the laser. Sixteen African nations become independent. Cyprus becomes independent.

1961 U.S. tries unsuccessfully to overthrow Castro in Cuba. Alan Shepard becomes first American to go into space. Communists build wall between East and West Berlin. Soviets are first to send man into space.

1962 Cuban missile crisis; President Kennedy orders blockade of Cuba to force Soviets to remove missles on Cuban soil. John Glenn is first American to orbit earth. Algeria gains independence from France.

1963 Dr. King gives his "I have a dream. . ." speech in Washington, D.C. President Kennedy is assassinated. Development of an effective measles vaccine. The Beatles enjoy unparalleled success as a music group in England and later the world. Government of Ngo Dinh Diem is toppled in South Vietnam.

1964 Tonkin Gulf Resolution gives President Johnson power to escalate America's role in Vietnam

War. Aleksei Kosygin becomes Soviet premier; Leonid Brezhnev becomes general secretary of the Communist party. Jawaharlal Nehru dies in India.

1965 Dr. King leads protest march from Selma to Montgomery, Alabama; he seeks an end to discrimination in voting registration. Voting Rights Act is passed in Congress. First American walks in space. Soviets make first space walk. Rhodesia declares its independence. Gambia gains independence. India and Pakistan fight over Kashmir.

1966 Petrofsky graduates from high school. Race riots in a number of major American cities including Chicago and Cleveland. Beginning of Cultural Revolution in China (1966-69). Indira Gandhi becomes prime minister of India.

1967 Peace talks begin in Paris between the U.S. and Hanoi. Antiwar protests begin. Dr. Christian Bernard of South Africa does first heart transplant on a human. Nguyen Van Thieu is elected president of South Vietnam. Six-Day War between Israel and several Arab states.

1968 Dr. King is assassinated in Memphis; riots break out in protest. Senator Robert Kennedy of New York is assassinated. Richard Nixon is elected president. Alexander Dubcek regime in Czechoslovakia, committed to reforms, is crushed by Soviets.

1969 America lands a man on the moon. Eight are indicted for conspiring to incite a riot at the Democratic National Convention of 1968, acquitted in 1970. Colonel Muammar al-Quadhafi becomes ruler of Libya. Golda Meir becomes prime minister of Israel.

1970 Four students are killed when National Guard troops fire into a crowd of antiwar protesters at Kent State University. Anwar al-Sadat becomes president of Egypt.

1971 Daniel Ellsberg publishes classified documents on U.S. involvement in Vietnam. For this, he is prosecuted, but acquitted. People's Republic of China admitted to the U.N.

1972 Watergate burglary occurs. President Nixon visits China. Apollo 17 mission, last manned moon landing. Nixon is reelected president. Arab terrorists kill Israeli athletes at Olympic Games in Munich. Martial law declared in Philippines.

1973 Watergate hearings investigate the president and key members of his staff regarding a cover-up of the Watergate burglary. Vice-president Agnew resigns after he is charged with income tax evasion. End of U.S. involvement in Vietnam War. Juan Peron is reelected president after returning to Argentina. Yom Kippur War between Israel and Arab neighbors. OPEC is formed.

1974 President Nixon resigns his office after nearly being impeached for his alleged part in the Watergate cover-up among other charges. Vice-president Gerald Ford becomes president, pardons Nixon for any possible wrong-doing he may have committed while president. Petrofsky earns Ph.D. in physiology. Peron dies and his wife, Isabel, becomes president. OPEC ends oil embargo against the U.S.

1975 Two assassination attempts on President Ford. Soviet bloc signs Helsinki Accord with the West which promotes peace and human rights. End of Vietnam War. Khmer Rouge take over Cambodia. Fighting between Muslims and Christians begins in Lebanon.

1976 U.S. celebrates its 200th birthday. Jimmy Carter elected president. Viking 1 and 2 land on Mars. A daughter, Melissa, is born to Petrofsky and wife. Isabel Peron is overthrown in Argentina. Chinese Premier Chou En-lai and Communist party Chairman Mao Tse-tung die. Hua Kuo-feng becomes premier and chairman.

1977 Voyager 1 and 2 are launched; eventual destination will be near Saturn and Jupiter. Menachem Begin becomes Israeli prime minister.

1978 U.S. establishes diplomatic relations with People's Republic of China. Camp David peace talks held between Egyptian President Anwar Sadat and Menachem Begin.

1979 Petrofsky transfers to Wright State University, becomes professor of physiology and biomedical engineering. President Somoza deposed by Sandinista guerrillas in Nicaragua. Israel and Egypt sign peace treaty. Revolution in Iran; Shah flees. U.S. embassy in Teheran taken over and 50 hostages held. Soviets invade Afghanistan.

1980 Ronald Reagan elected president. Solidarity, Polish trade union, established with Lech Walesa as its leader. Shah of Iran dies of cancer in Cairo. Civil war in Cambodia.

1981 Ronald Reagan takes office and hostages in Iran are released at same time. Attempted assassination of president. Martial law declared in Poland. President Sadat assassinated.

1982 Therapeutic Technologies Inc. is founded. Nan Davis stands for first time since her accident, later walks. War in El Salvador between left-wing guerrillas and government forces. War in Falkland Islands between Britain and Argentina. Israel invades Lebanon.

1983 Nan Davis walks to receive her college diploma. Susan Steele takes her first steps since her accident. U.S. invades Grenada. Lech Walesa wins Nobel Peace Prize. Acquino Benigno assassinated in Philippines. Soviets shoot down civilian Korean jetliner. Over 200 soldiers in U.S. peacekeeping force massacred in Lebanon in suicide bombing raid.

INDEX- *Page numbers in boldface type indicate illustrations.*

111